THE LOVE ONE A

SUBMITTING
LETTING GOD USE OTHERS TO LEAD ME

A Bible Study by

MINISTERING TO THE CHURCHES OF THE WORLD
600 Meridian Avenue, Suite 200
San Jose, California 95126-3427

Published by

BRINGING TRUTH TO LIFE
NavPress Publishing Group
P.O. Box 35001, Colorado Springs, Colorado 80935

© 1979, 1990 by Churches Alive
Revised edition © 1993
All rights reserved. No part of this publication
  may be reproduced in any form without
  written permission from NavPress, P.O. Box
  35001, Colorado Springs, CO 80935.
ISBN 08910-97864

Cover photograph: Willard Clay
Interior cartoons: Bob Fuller

Unless otherwise identified, all Scripture quotations in this publication are taken from the
HOLY BIBLE: NEW INTERNATIONAL VERSION®
(NIV®). Copyright © 1973, 1978, 1984 by
International Bible Society. Used by permission
of Zondervan Publishing House. All rights
reserved.

Printed in the United States of America

Because we share kindred aims for helping local churches fulfill Christ's Great Commission to "go and make disciples," NavPress and Churches Alive have joined efforts on certain strategic publishing projects that are intended to bring effective disciplemaking resources into the service of the local church.

For more than a decade, Churches Alive has teamed up with churches of all denominations to establish vigorous disciplemaking ministries. At the same time, NavPress has focused on publishing Bible studies, books, and other resources that have grown out of The Navigators' 50 years of disciplemaking experience.

Now, together, we're working to offer special products like this one that are designed to stimulate a deeper, more fruitful commitment to Christ in the local gatherings of His Church.

The LOVE ONE ANOTHER *series was written by Russ Korth, Ron Wormser, Jr., and Ron Wormser, Sr. of Churches Alive. Many individuals from both Churches Alive and NavPress contributed greatly in bringing this project to publication.*

Contents

LESSON ONE: **The Sovereignty of God** — 5
LESSON TWO: **The Nature of Submission** — 9
LESSON THREE: **Good Leadership** — 15
LESSON FOUR: **The Responsibility of Leaders** — 19
LESSON FIVE: **Submitting at Work** — 25
LESSON SIX: **Submitting to Government** — 31
LESSON SEVEN: **Submission in the Family** — 37
LESSON EIGHT: **Submitting to Spiritual Leaders** — 43

Some people want authority to force their desires on others.
But God has other reasons for authority.

Lesson One
The Sovereignty of God

1 Use a dictionary or other reference material to define "sovereignty."

2 Study Colossians 1:16-17 and write a short paragraph about God's sovereignty.

3 How does the fact that God is sovereign make you feel?

4 How is God's sovereignty revealed in each of the following passages?

Exodus 3:19-20

Isaiah 45:5-7

Romans 9:14-21

5 What authority does God's Word have?

Isaiah 55:11

Jeremiah 23:28-29

Hebrews 4:12 (kjv—"quick" = "living")

6 Read Acts 4. Describe how the confidence the early believers had in the sovereignty of God is revealed in each of the following.

a. In what they did.

b. In what they said.

c. In what they prayed. (Verses 24-30)

7 What are some ways your confidence in God's sovereignty affects your family or church life?

8 What example did Job set in responding to God's sovereignty? (Job 40:1-5, 42:1-6)

9 What are some of the ways God expresses His sovereignty in the affairs of people?

Lesson Two
The Nature of Submission

▼

1 Briefly relate a positive experience you have had by submitting to an authority over you.

2 What concepts are associated with submission in the following verses?

Ephesians 6:5-6

Titus 2:9

Titus 3:1-2

3 Using the information from question 2, write a short paragraph explaining what it means to submit.

4 What did Jesus teach about submission in Matthew 21:28-32?

5 Do you think submission means obeying without question? Explain.

6 Read Romans 8:5-7.

    a. What are the two states of mind presented in this passage?

b. Can you conclude that the other state of mind produces submission? Explain.

c. Which state of mind produces rebellion?

7 Describe the kind of person to whom you should voluntarily submit. (1 Corinthians 16:15-16; KJV—"addicted" = "devoted")

8 How do you benefit when you submit to people who have been placed over you? (1 Peter 5:5-6)

9 Why is submitting to authority essential to eliminating frustration from your life?

10 What do you see to be the difference, if any, between obeying and submitting?

Having authority does not mean sitting on a throne with no cares. Authority means you have responsibility to those over whom you have authority as well as to God and to those who appointed you.

Lesson Three
Good Leadership

1 Who was the best supervisor you have ever had? What made this supervisor so good?

2 What traits characterize good leadership? (2 Samuel 23:3-4)

3 What other qualities are necessary for good leadership?

Proverbs 12:24 (KJV—"tribute" = "forced labor")

Proverbs 17:7

Proverbs 24:23

4 Choose one of the above characteristics and explain more fully why you think it is necessary for good leadership.

5 What are two bad leadership traits and the results of them?

Proverbs 28:16 (KJV—"wanteth" = "lacks")

Proverbs 29:12

6 What special standard does Proverbs 31:4-5 suggest for leaders? Why?

7 Rewrite 2 Corinthians 3:4-6 in your own words and fit it to your own situation, using "parent," "boss," "husband," "Sunday school teacher," or another position of authority you may hold.

8 a. Read Matthew 23:1-12. What are some of the wrong motives people have in seeking authority?

b. List at least three of Jesus' teachings about authority.

9 What are some practical steps that can help develop good leaders in a local church?

Lesson Four
The Responsibility of Leaders

1 Which do you think is easier, leading or following? Explain.

2 a. What should a leader's concern be? (2 Chronicles 19:6)

b. What are some ways this concern will be demonstrated? (2 Chronicles 19:7)

3 Read Ezekiel 34:2-10. List the responsibilities God indicates that shepherds have to sheep. Next to each responsibility shepherds have, list a similar responsibility which any leader has to his followers.

RESPONSIBILITY OF SHEPHERDS	RESPONSIBILITY OF LEADERS
Feed the flock	*Meet needs of followers*

4 a. Jesus also used the shepherd as an illustration of leadership. What principles of leadership did He teach in John 10:11-14?

b. How can you apply these principles in your church relationships?

5 a. What principle did Jesus teach about responsibility to followers? (Matthew 20:26-28)

b. What are some ways Paul followed this teaching? (1 Thessalonians 2:3-12)

6 Adapt the commands that Moses gave leaders in Deuteronomy 17:14-20 to today.

7 What warning did James give about having a position of authority? (James 3:1)

8 As you consider the position of authority you have, review the teachings of this lesson and record some specific actions you can take to improve your leadership.

9 How should you respond to a leader who does not fulfill his responsibility? (Matthew 23:2-4)

Submission does not mean losing your self-identity, but putting yourself in a position to experience God's power within you.

Lesson Five
Submitting at Work

▼

1 List at least three important factors that make a job enjoyable.

2 Paul addressed Ephesians 6:5-8 to slaves. Rewrite this passage as you think Paul would address it to employees today.

3 Why should you submit to your boss at work?

4 What are some standards you should maintain at your job? After each one, mention one way you could apply this standard.

Proverbs 21:25-26

Colossians 3:23-24

Hebrews 13:5 (KJV—"conversation" = "manner of life")

5 Why do you think the wrong attitude toward money as described in Ecclesiastes 5:10-11 and 1 Timothy 6:9-10 might make it difficult for you to be submissive in your job?

6 If you feel your supervisor is high-handed and insensitive and you find it difficult to submit, what do the following verses suggest you do instead of complaining?

Psalm 41:11

1 Peter 5:6-7

7 What is the proper way of registering a complaint?

8 During coffee break several of your friends begin complaining about the boss and some recent decisions he has made.

a. What do you think you are likely to do?

b. What should you do and/or say?

9 Read Genesis 39. What lessons about submitting at work are illustrated in this passage?

10 How should you determine when you are not going to submit at work? What should you do?

Church leaders are not God's policemen on earth to keep us all in line. They exercise authority for the well-being of the entire church.

Lesson Six
Submitting to Government

1 An inscription on the wall of one government building reads: "The proper function of government is to make it easy for people to do good and difficult for people to do evil." Write an inscription you would like to see on the wall of a government building.

2 How is God's sovereignty expressed in government? (Psalm 75:6-7)

3 a. According to Colossians 1:16-18, for what purposes do people in power have their authority?

b. Do you think these purposes are being fulfilled? Explain.

4 Read Romans 13:1-7.

a. What is the *basic* reason you should submit to civil authority?

b. List two *practical* reasons to submit to civil authority.

c. What attitudes should you have toward those in power?

5 Why can you submit to people in full assurance that your interests will be protected?

Proverbs 21:1

Lamentations 3:37

6 a. What do you think Peter means in 1 Peter 2:15-16 when he says you are free?

b. How does this freedom relate to your submission to civil authority? (1 Peter 2:13-17)

7 a. What did Jesus say about authority in John 19:10-11?

b. How did He apply this view of authority? (1 Peter 2:23)

8 Read Acts 5:27-29 and 1 Peter 2:13-16.

    a. When should you not obey an authority?

    b. Why should you obey an authority even though it may be difficult or inconvenient for you?

9 How can you follow the example of Daniel when he felt he could not submit to the king? (Daniel 1:8-16)

10 Read Matthew 17:24-27. The tax Jesus and Peter were being asked to pay was the temple tax as prescribed in Exodus 30:13. From Jesus' reply to Peter, answer the questions that follow.

    a. Who is the "King" of the temple?

b. Who is the "Son" of the "King"?

c. Who, then, should be exempt from the tax?

d. Why did Jesus pay the tax?

e. What is one principle this example illustrates?

11 What is the proper way to attempt to change laws you consider unjust or immoral?

Lesson Seven
Submission in the Family

1 What emotions are elicited in you when you hear the phrase, "We are family!"?

2 What are some practical reasons children should obey their parents?

Proverbs 3:1-4

Ephesians 6:1-3

3 Read Luke 2:41-51. What lessons can be learned from the example of Jesus as a boy?

4 a. Read 1 Samuel 2:12-17. What were Eli's children like?

b. Read 1 Samuel 3:11-14. Why did God judge Eli?

c. What was God's judgment?

5 What are some things you think parents could do to help keep their children from becoming like Eli's children?

6 a. Study Ephesians 5:21-28 and complete the following:

Husbands and wives should . . .

Husbands should . . .

Wives should . . .

b. From your study of Ephesians 5:21-28 complete the following: The husband is head of the wife because (check all correct answers) . . .

☐ He is better.
☐ He thinks more clearly.
☐ He is less emotional.
☐ He can handle the responsibility, and the wife can't.
☐ He is more important than a woman.
☐ He is assigned this responsibility.

Husbands are to (check all correct answers) . . .

☐ Keep their wives in line.
☐ Sacrificially love their wives.
☐ Make *all* decisions.
☐ Care for and protect their wives.

c. What advantages are there to husbands when they sacrificially love their wives?

d. What advantages are there to wives when they submit to their husbands?

7 What additional information regarding submission in the family is given in 1 Peter 3:1-6?

8 Peter cited Sarah as an example to emulate. What do you think makes her a good role model?

9 When do you think a husband should submit to his wife?

There are many roles that you play in life.
God has established lines of authority in each one.

Lesson Eight
Submitting to Spiritual Leaders

▼

1 What people do you consider to be your spiritual leaders?

2 What attitudes should you have toward your church leaders?

1 Thessalonians 5:12-13

1 Peter 5:5-6

3 How do you think Jesus' admonition in Matthew 23:1-3 should be applied today?

4 List the commands which are given in Hebrews 13:17 along with the reason for the commands.

COMMAND	REASON

5 The Bible commands you to consider the outcome of your church leaders' lives (Hebrews 13:7). Why is this so important? (Luke 6:40; KJV—"perfect" = "mature")

6 Complete the following statement: *Because of my commitment to the Lord, I am supportive of my church leaders. I feel I can best serve them and the church by . . .*

7 How would you respond if your pastor came to you and said, "The other church leaders and I have prayed about it extensively and feel it is God's will for you to teach one of the Sunday school classes this quarter"?

8 Read Acts 15:1-22.

   a. What was the problem?

   b. How was it handled?

   c. How was submission or lack of it revealed?

   d. How did Peter use his authority?

e. What lessons do you feel can be learned from this episode?

9 Read 1 Samuel 14:6-14.

a. What attitudes do you see evidenced in the life of Jonathan's armor bearer? How were they evidenced?

ATTITUDE	HOW EVIDENCED

b. What relationship do you think there is between the armor bearer's attitudes and the results he and Jonathan saw?

c. How can you copy his example in your church situation?

10 Read Numbers 16:1-35.

a. Who was the God-appointed leader?

b. Who rebelled? (Verses 1-3)

c. What positions of leadership did they hold? (Verse 2)

d. What reason did they give for rebelling? (Verses 3,13-14)

e. What was God's evaluation of these men? (Verses 23-35)

f. How do you think Korah and his friends could have been submissive and still expressed their ideas?

Churches Alive!

This study is just one item in a wide range of small group material authored by Churches Alive. Continue your study with other books in this series.

Churches Alive has local representatives who provide their own living expenses to serve you at your church. On-site support and training conferences will develop commitment and vision in group leaders. Our experienced staff can help you develop leaders, enrich your groups, and reach out to others.

Conferences and Support Services

A Pastor's Perspective:

"Churches Alive was a tremendous help to us when we were getting started in our discipleship ministry. We had to make a choice—either try to learn ourselves and make a lot of mistakes, or get some help and minimize mistakes. Their careful but goal-oriented approach helps any church build a solid, perpetuating ministry."

Churches Alive!
600 Meridian Avenue
Suite 200
San Jose, CA 95126
(408) 294-6000
(408) 294-6029 FAX

Conferences

Designed to strengthen the effectiveness of your leaders, our conferences and seminars range from one to four days. Most are taught by Churches Alive staff and local pastors. In addition, we arrange special seminars in your church to encourage people in your church to study the Bible.

Support Services

In dozens of denominations, our staff helps churches large and small. We can help you evaluate, plan, train leaders, and expand your small groups. Invite a Churches Alive representative to explore small group discipleship at your church.

Call 1-800-755-3787